My *Little* *Brother*

by Hayden Woods
Illustrated by Gloria Calderas

Glenview, Illinois • Boston, Massachusetts • Chandler, Arizona
Upper Saddle River, New Jersey

mother

"You will have a little brother,"
Mother says.
I am excited!

2

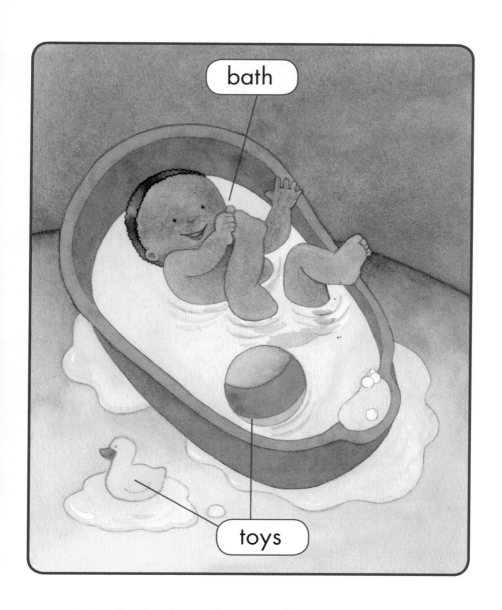

bath

toys

My little brother will need help.
I will help give him a bath.
We will play with toys.

3

We will grow.
We will walk together.

We will feed the birds.
We will play with blocks.

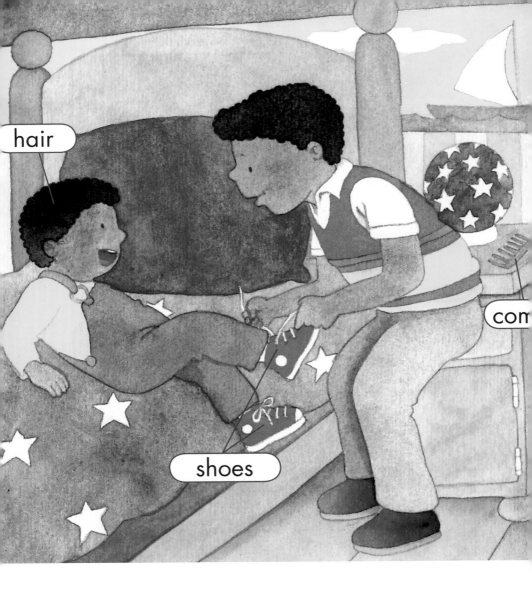

hair

shoes

com

I will tie his shoes.
I will comb his hair.

We will read stories.
We will laugh together.

We will go to bed.
I will love my little brother!